Birds

CHELSEA CLUBHOUSE

An Imprint of Chelsea House Publishers

A Haights Cross Communications Company

Philadelphia

June Loves

Chelsea Clubhouse
1974 Sproul Road, Suite 400
Broomall, PA 19008-0914

The Chelsea House world wide web address is www.chelseahouse.com

Library of Congress Cataloging-in-Publication Data

Loves, June.
    Birds / June Loves.
    v. cm. — (Pets)

    Contents: Birds — Kinds of birds — Parts of a bird — Feathers —Young birds — Choosing pet birds — Caring for pet birds — Feeding — Cleaning — Training — Visiting the vet — Pet bird clubs — In the wild.

    ISBN 0-7910-7547-8
    1. Cage birds—Juvenile literature. [1. Birds as pets. 2. Pets.] I. Title. II. Series: Loves, June. Pets.
    SF461.35 .L68 2004
    636.6′8—dc21

                                                                2002155663

First published in 2003 by
MACMILLAN EDUCATION AUSTRALIA PTY LTD
627 Chapel Street, South Yarra, Australia, 3141

Associated companies and representatives throughout the world.

Copyright © June Loves 2003
Copyright in photographs © individual photographers as credited

Page layout by Domenic Lauricella
Photo research by Legend Images

Printed in China

Acknowledgements
The author and the publisher are grateful to the following for permission to reproduce copyright material:

Cover photograph: girl finger-taming pet bird, courtesy of ANT Photo Library.

ANT Photo Library, pp. 1, 10, 22, 23, 24, 27, 30; Roger Brown/Auscape, p. 17; Gary Steer/Auscape, p. 29; Jason Edwards/Bio-Images, p. 12; Nigel Clements, pp. 4, 25; Lloyd Franklin, p. 21; L & O Schick/Naturefocus, p. 14 (bottom); Dave Watts/Naturefocus, p. 15 (top); Pelusey Photography, p. 19 (bucket & scrubbing brush); Photography Ebiz, pp. 6, 7, 8–9, 11, 14 (top), 15 (bottom), 16, 18–19, 28; Dale Mann/Retrospect, pp. 5, 13, 26; Sarah Saunders, p. 20.

While every care has been taken to trace and acknowledge copyright, the publisher tenders their apologies for any accidental infringement where copyright has proved untraceable. Where the attempt has been unsuccessful, the publisher welcomes information that would redress the situation.

Contents

Birds

Birds are lovable pets. They are good pets for people who live in apartments or small houses. Parakeets are popular pet birds.

This type of parakeet is called a budgie.

This large cage is called an aviary.

Some pet birds live in cages indoors. Others can be kept in **aviaries** outside. Pet birds need food, water, space to fly, and care every day.

Kinds of Birds

There are many kinds of birds. They can be different sizes, shapes, and colors.

Pet ducks need a place to swim.

Different **breeds** of birds have different features.

- ✪ Male canaries sing beautifully.
- ✪ Zebra finches are small and attractive.
- ✪ Homing pigeons can find their own way home.
- ✪ Pet parakeets, such as budgies, can be different colors.
- ✪ Ducks have webbed feet for paddling in the water.

These birds are zebra finches.

Birds are the only animals with feathers.

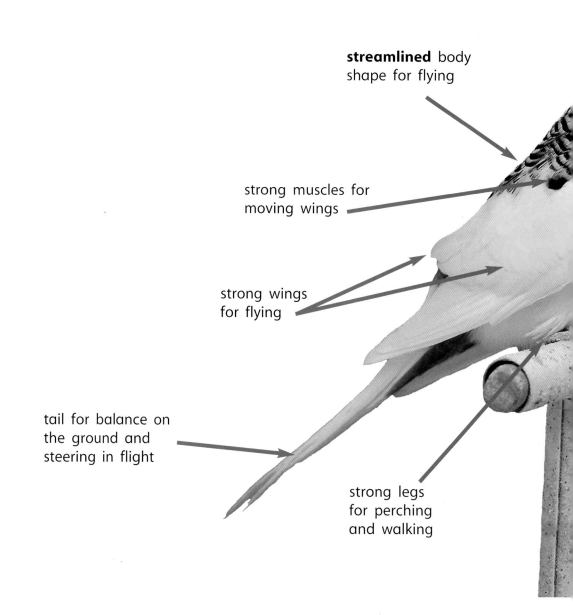

streamlined body shape for flying

strong muscles for moving wings

strong wings for flying

tail for balance on the ground and steering in flight

strong legs for perching and walking

sharp ears for
hearing danger

sharp eyes to see

short, hooked beak
for cracking seeds

four claws to hold
onto perches

9

Feathers

Feathers protect birds and keep them warm. A bird's feathers are called plumage.

soft **down** feathers keep the bird warm

body and flight feathers make a smooth surface

tail feathers help the bird steer in the air and balance on the ground

Each feather has a **shaft** down the center. Thin branches called **barbs** grow from the shaft. The barbs have tiny hooks that connect them to each other. Feathers fit together to make a smooth surface for flying.

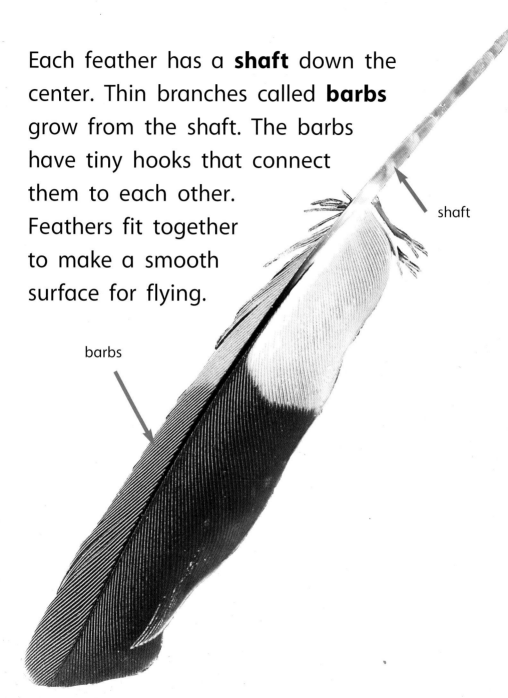

shaft

barbs

11

Molting

Birds **molt** at least once a year. New feathers grow to replace old ones. Pet birds can look untidy and ragged when they are molting. This does not mean they are sick.

These blue-and-yellow macaws are molting.

Preening

A bird uses its beak to **preen**, or comb, its feathers. It also spreads a thin layer of oil to waterproof its feathers.

During preening, a bird combs its feathers into shape.

Young Birds

The female bird lays eggs with hard shells. Wild birds make nests for their eggs. Pet birds lay eggs in nest boxes.

Baby birds hatch from the eggs after a few weeks. Their eyes are shut. They are helpless.

As they grow, young birds become covered in down.

Young birds develop inside the eggs. Baby birds are called chicks.

Young birds usually stay in the nest. Their parents feed and protect them.

Young birds leave the nest when they are big enough to fly and find their own food.

Choosing Pet Birds

Choose pet birds that have bright eyes and clean feathers. They should have well-formed beaks and claws that perch firmly. Make sure your cage is the right size for the birds you choose.

Larger birds need bigger cages.

Budgies are ready to leave their parents for a new home when they are between six and eight weeks old. You can choose male or female budgies.

cere

A male budgie has a bright blue **cere** across his nostrils. A female budgie has a brown cere.

Caring for Pet Birds

Set up a cage before you bring pet birds home. These are some supplies you need to care for your pet birds.

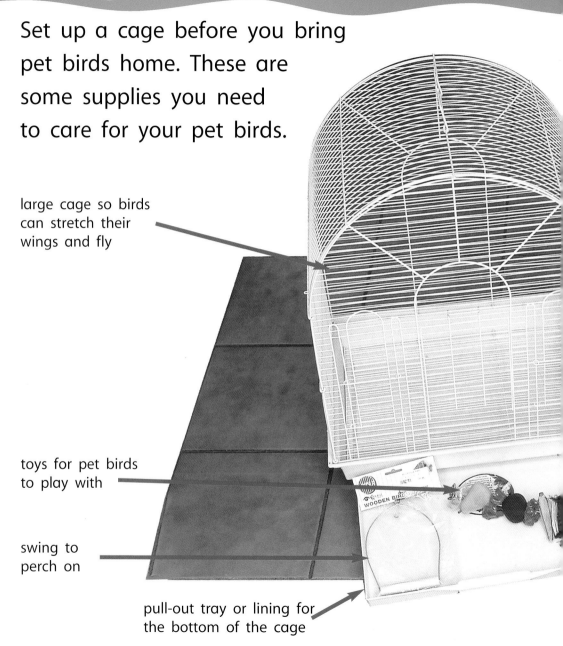

large cage so birds can stretch their wings and fly

toys for pet birds to play with

swing to perch on

pull-out tray or lining for the bottom of the cage

Pet birds enjoy playing with toys in their cage. You can buy toys such as balls, swings, mirrors, bells, and ladders from a pet shop.

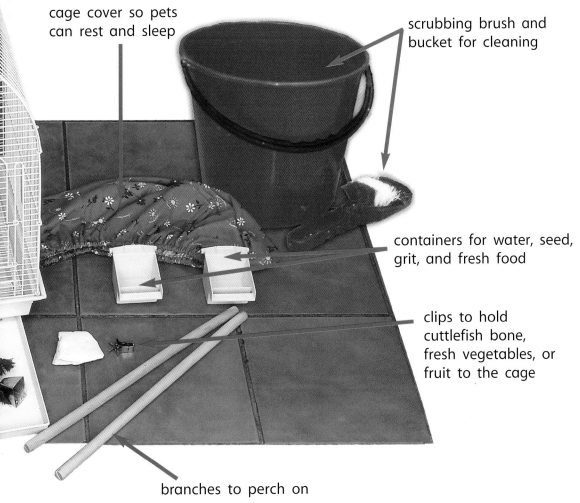

cage cover so pets can rest and sleep

scrubbing brush and bucket for cleaning

containers for water, seed, grit, and fresh food

clips to hold cuttlefish bone, fresh vegetables, or fruit to the cage

branches to perch on

Bath time

Birds like to have baths, especially on hot days. Place a flat bowl of **lukewarm** water in the cage. Pet birds will splash around and then shake their feathers dry.

Baths help pet birds to clean their feathers and to stay cool.

Keeping birds in an aviary

You can keep more than two birds in an outdoor aviary. An outdoor aviary should give birds shelter and a large area for flying.

An outdoor aviary provides lots of room for birds to fly.

Feeding

Pet birds need fresh seed every day. You can buy food from a pet store or supermarket. Store the food in an airtight container to keep it fresh and clean.

Give your birds fresh food every day.

Cuttlefish bone is attached to the cage. A bird may chew it or rub its beak on it.

Make sure pet birds have clean water to drink every day. Shell grit and cuttlefish bone provide **calcium** to make your bird's beak and bones strong. They also keep its **digestive system** healthy. Treat birds to fresh vegetables, fruit, and grasses.

Cleaning

The cage needs to be cleaned each week.
Keep your pets safe when you clean
their cage.

The cage

⚙ Use warm, soapy water to clean and scrub
the tray and cage bars.

⚙ Replace the tray lining, or add sawdust or
sand to catch the droppings.

Add fresh litter or lining
when you clean the cage.

Food and water containers

✪ Use warm, soapy water to clean the food and water containers.

✪ Rinse containers well before putting them back in the cage.

Use a brush to clean out food and water containers.

Training

You can teach some birds to talk. Choose simple words, and repeat them over and over again. Pet birds can also be trained to whistle or **mimic** sounds.

Some birds can be taught to repeat simple words.

A young budgie can be trained to sit on a person's finger.

Train your bird to perch on your finger.
When it is used to this, you can let it fly
around the room and return to your finger.
Be sure to shut windows and doors.

Visiting the Vet

The **vet** will help to keep your pet bird healthy. Take your pet bird to the vet for regular check-ups. If your pet looks sick, take it to the vet for treatment.

Use a cage to take your pet bird to the vet's office.

Pet Bird Clubs

If you join a pet bird club, you can share handy hints and useful information with other club members. Many clubs have competitions and other activities for members.

Birds that have the best features receive awards at bird shows.

In the Wild

In the wild, budgies live in flocks. The female budgie lays her eggs in the hollow of a tree. The male budgie helps her look after the young birds.

Wild budgies are mostly green.

Glossary

aviaries	large, enclosed outdoor areas to keep pet birds in
barbs	thin branches of a feather; each barb has tiny hooks that connect to other barbs
breeds	animals that belong to the same scientific group and have a similar appearance
calcium	a substance found in limestone, chalk, or bone that plants and animals need to grow strong bones
cere	a soft, waxy swelling at the top of a bird's beak
digestive system	parts inside a bird's stomach that process food
down	very soft, fine feathers
lukewarm	slightly warm
mimic	to copy sounds or voices
molt	to lose feathers
preen	to clean and smooth feathers
shaft	a hollow tube at the center of a feather
streamlined	shaped to move easily through the air
vet	a doctor who treats animals; short for veterinarian

Index